Footballs

BEFORE THE STORE

BY RACHEL LYNETTE • ILLUSTRATED BY DAN McGEEHAN

Published by The Child's World®
1980 Lookout Drive • Mankato, MN 56003-1705
800-599-READ • www.childsworld.com

ACKNOWLEDGMENTS
The Child's World®: Mary Berendes, Publishing Director
The Design Lab: Design and production
Red Line Editorial: Editorial direction
Content Consultant: S. Jack Hu, Ph.D., J. Reid and Polly Anderson Professor of Manufacturing Technology,
Professor of Mechanical Engineering and Industrial and Operations Engineering, The University of Michigan

ISBN 9781609736750
LCCN 2011940072

PHOTO CREDITS
Nick M. Do/iStockphoto, cover, 1; Sergiy Palamarchuk/Dreamstime, cover (inset), 1 (inset); David Lee/
Shutterstock Images, 5, 13, 25; Jim Parkin/Shutterstock Images, 7; Josh Laverty/iStockphoto, 11; Chimpin-
ski/Dreamstime, 15, 30 (top); Radojko Maksimovic/iStockphoto, 17; Falk Kienas/iStockphoto, 24; Studio
1One/Shutterstock Images, 29, 31 (bottom)

Design elements: Nick M. Do/iStockphoto

Printed in the United States of America

ABOUT THE AUTHOR

Rachel Lynette has written more than 100 books for children, as well as teacher resources. She also writes blogs for teachers. Rachel lives near Seattle, Washington, where the Seahawks play. She has a daughter in high school and a son in college.

Contents

CHAPTER ONE

A Funny-Shaped Ball!

Have you ever thrown a football? It is fun to toss back and forth with a friend. Some people play on football teams. And many people enjoy watching football games. People have been playing football for more than 100 years.

Why isn't a football round like most balls? The almond shape of a football is just right for throwing long distances. It is also easier to tuck under your arm and carry than a round ball. These are both

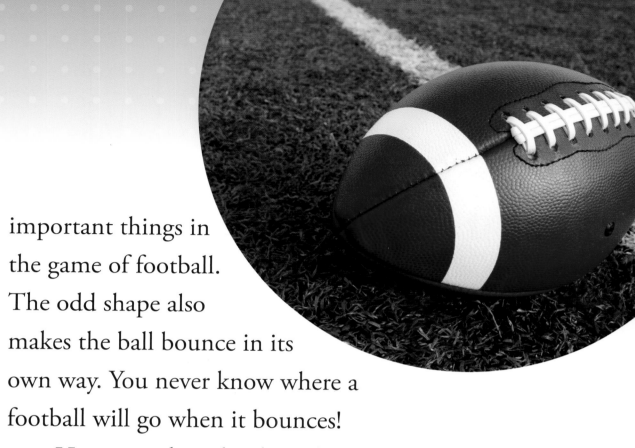

important things in the game of football. The odd shape also makes the ball bounce in its own way. You never know where a football will go when it bounces!

Have you thought about how footballs are made? There are many steps. It starts with the outside of the ball. This comes from a cowhide. A football's covering is very important. It keeps a football in its funny shape!

Footballs have an almond shape.

CHAPTER TWO

At the Football Factory

Most footballs are made from cowhides. Cheaper footballs may be made from rubber or plastic. The cowhides are large pieces of dried cow skin. Before the football factory, a few things happen to the hides. First they are **tanned**. This keeps the skins from cracking. Hides that are tanned are called **leather**. They are also stamped with a bumpy texture. It makes the football easier to grip. Most of the hides are also dyed brown.

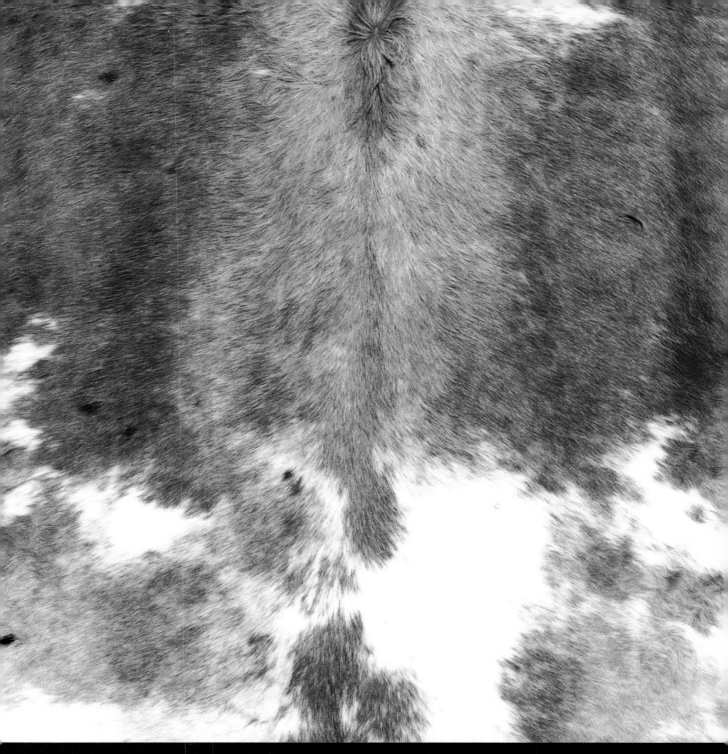

Cowhides are tanned to make leather.

The hides are cut into four almond-shaped panels. Each panel is the same size.

Footballs are sometimes called pigskins. The first footballs were made from pig **bladders**!

A worker called a cutter places a metal pattern on the hide. The metal pattern is a bit like a large cookie cutter. The cutter then uses a machine to press the metal pattern into the hide. This cuts the panel into the almond shape. The cutter uses as much of the hide as possible. Panels for ten footballs can be cut from one cowhide.

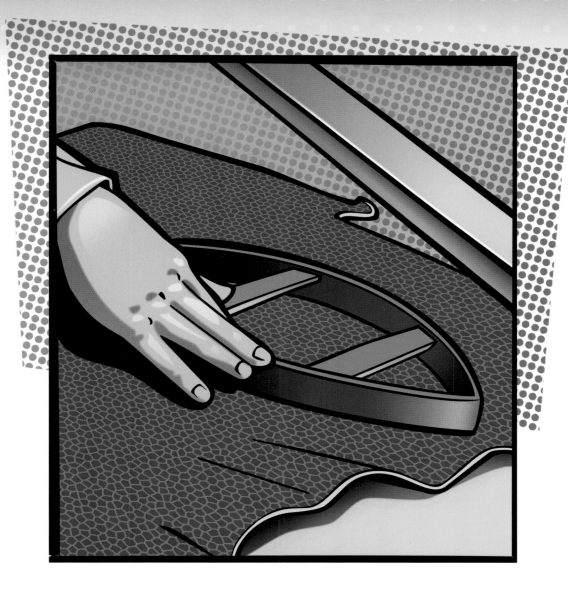

A worker cuts hide into football panels.

CHAPTER THREE

Stamping and Painting

Have you seen the words and pictures on a football? They show the **logo** and name of the company that made the football. They are stamped onto the panels before a football is put together. A stamping machine prints on one or two of the panels. Other markings may also be stamped on some of the panels. Balls that are used for the National Football League (NFL) are always stamped with the NFL logo. They also show the signature of the NFL commissioner. The commissioner is the president of the NFL.

All of the footballs that are used for the NFL are made by Wilson Sporting Goods in Ada, Ohio.

Balls that are used for the NFL have its logo.

Next the panels are made thinner. Each one is run through a machine. It peels off a layer of leather from the back. Each panel must have the same thickness. This helps every football have the same weight.

A thick white line is painted at each end of two panels. A worker puts a panel on a machine. Then the machine paints the lines. When the ball is done, the white lines will be on the front half of the football. The lines help football players see the ball. Some footballs have lines that go all the way around. For those footballs, all four panels must be painted. Other footballs have no lines at all. NFL footballs do not have lines.

Some footballs have white lines painted on them.

CHAPTER FOUR

Putting Footballs Together

Footballs get kicked around a lot, so they need to be strong. Leather is strong, but it is not strong enough. Linings are added to make the football stronger. The linings are made from cotton and **vinyl**. They are sewn to the backs of all four panels. The linings are the same shape and size as the panels. It only takes a few seconds for a worker to sew on the lining. The lining also keeps the football from stretching out of shape.

*Football **seams** show where the panels were sewn together.*

Next a hole is made for the **air gauge** on one of the panels. The air gauge is important. It is used to add air to the football. Sometimes footballs get soft. This happens when they run low on air. Eight holes are punched into two of the panels. They are made for the laces. A machine punches all eight holes at once. They go at the edges of the panels.

How do these four separate panels become a football? That happens when the four panels are sewn together. A special, powerful sewing machine is used. The panels are sewn together inside out. The stitches will not show when the football is done. The only part that is not sewn is the part with the lace holes.

A machine punches holes for the laces and air gauge.

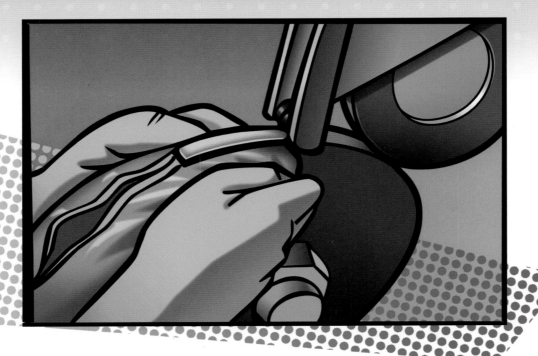

Next the seams need to be flattened. This makes it so the football will not be lumpy. The seams are pressed down with a roller. This is a little like the way you roll cookie dough with a rolling pin. A special press makes the seams flat on the ends of the football.

The seams are flattened with a machine.

CHAPTER FIVE

Right-Side Out

Now the four panels of leather have the shape of a football. But, the football is still inside out. Have you ever heard of a football taking a bath? Every football takes a 15-second steam bath. Then it is turned right-side out. The bath makes the leather soft. Leather is easier to shape and move when it is soft.

Turning a football right-side out is not an easy job. The leather is still tough. The person who does this step is called the ball turner. The ball turner must be very strong. He or she uses a pole that sticks up from a table. First the ball turner puts the football on top of the pole. The opening with the lace holes is at the top. Then the worker pulls the opening of the football down over the pole. This turns the football right-side out. Next the end of the pole is pushed through against the insides of the football. This gives the football the right shape.

A worker turns the football right-side out.

CHAPTER SIX

Lacing It Up

Inside every football is a bladder. It is made from a stretchy plastic. The bladder holds air inside the football. It is a bit like a very strong balloon. The empty bladder is pushed into the football though the opening of the ball. The air gauge on the bladder is pushed out through the air gauge hole. Then the end of the air gauge is clipped off so it will not stick out. Finally, the ball is **inflated** with air. The football is firm but still a little soft. It still needs to be laced.

Laces close the opening of a football.

The football is held in place with a clamp so it can be laced. The worker who does this is called a lacer. The lacer uses a tool called an **awl**. The awl looks like a screwdriver with a hole at the end. It is a little like a large sewing needle. The lacer pushes the awl through two holes on the football. Then the lace is threaded through the hole at the end of the awl. The lacer pulls the awl back through the holes. The lace is pulled with the awl.

One lacer can lace about 200 footballs in a single day!

The football is laced using a special tool called an awl.

The lace is a single strip of vinyl or leather just over 3 feet (1 m) long. The lace is threaded through each hole. Then it is run between the two rows of holes twice. Then it is laced through all the holes again. This holds the two strips in the center in place. The lacing closes the hole in the football. This also gives the player a good grip when throwing the ball.

The laces go through the holes and up the middle of a football

CHAPTER SEVEN

Inflating the Ball

Next the footballs are ready to be inflated. Each football is put into a steel **mold**. The mold is closed and the football is inflated with a bit too much air. This helps make sure that each football is the perfect shape. Before the football is removed from the mold, the extra air is released. Now the ball has the right amount of **air pressure** and is done!

Footballs for NFL games are inspected to be sure that they are perfect. An inspector weighs and measures each ball. Then each football's laces are checked.

Footballs are then put into boxes. They are ready
to be shipped to schools and stores.

The football is inflated with air.

CHAPTER EIGHT

Footballs for You

Footballs may travel by truck, by train, or both. Some footballs are made in other countries, such as China. These footballs travel to the United States by cargo ship before they go onto trains or trucks. A football may travel a long way to make it to the store!

Most footballs do not go to professional teams. Factories make footballs for college and high school teams, youth football teams, and people who just want to play with friends. The finished footballs are sent to stores. Sporting goods stores are great places to find footballs!

It is fun to play football with friends at school or at the park. Next time you hold a football in your hands, take a closer look. Can you feel the tiny bumps on the cowhide? Can you see where the four pieces were sewn together? Can you see how the ball was laced closed? This all makes a football easier to hold and throw. Now go score a touchdown!

Finally, the football is ready to toss around in the backyard!

FOOTBALL MAP

1 CUT PANELS

2 SEW PANELS

5 LACE THE BALL

3

SEAMS ARE FLATTENED

4

TURN THE BALL RIGHT-SIDE OUT

7

INTO YOUR HANDS

6

INFLATE THE BALL

31

GLOSSARY

air gauge (AIR GAYJ): An air gauge is a tool that measures air pressure. A hole is made in the panel for the air gauge.

air pressure (air PRESH-ur): Air pressure is the force that air in a space puts on the sides of the container. The air pressure has to be right in a football.

awl (AWL): An awl is a sharp metal tool for making holes in leather or wood. A worker uses an awl to make a football.

bladders (BLAD-urz): Bladders are soft bags that can hold air or parts of the body that hold waste liquid. Inside footballs are bladders.

inflated (in-FLATE-ed): To be inflated is to be filled with air. The bladder is inflated with air.

leather (leTH-ur): Leather is animal skin that has been tanned and is used to make products. Footballs are made with leather.

logo (LOH-goh): A logo is a symbol that stands for a company. On the outside of the football is a logo.

mold (MOHLD): A mold is a hollow container that you put something into to set its shape. Inside a mold, a football is filled with air.

seams (SEEMZ): Seams are the lines where two pieces of material have been sewn together. Football seams have to be flat.

tanned (TAND): Animal skin is tanned when it is soaked in liquids to make it into leather. Cowhides are tanned to make leather.

vinyl (VYE-nuhl): Vinyl is a light and very strong kind of plastic that is used to make products. Vinyl is used for football laces.

BOOKS

Buckley, James, Jr. *Scholastic Ultimate Guide to Football*. New York: Scholastic, 2010.

Gibbons, Gail. *My Football Book*. New York: HarperCollins, 2000.

Jacob, Greg. *The Everything Kids' Football Book*. Avon, MA: Adams Media, Inc., 2010.

Thomas, Keltie. *How Football Works*. Berkeley, CA: Maple Tree Press, 2010.

INDEX

Visit our Web site for links about football production: childsworld.com/links

Note to Parents, Teachers, and Librarians: We routinely verify our Web links to make sure they are safe and active sites. So encourage your readers to check them out!